D0948679

PESO
Sort It by WEIGHT

By Nicholas O'Hara
Traducido por Eida de la Vega

Gareth Stevens
PUBLISHING

conceptos
básicos

Agrupar significa juntar cosas que son parecidas. Puedes agrupar cosas que sean livianas o pesadas.

Sorting is putting things that are alike together. You can sort things that are light and heavy.

3

Algunas cosas
son pesadas.

Some things are heavy.

Algunas cosas
son livianas.

Some things are light.

Las aves pueden ser
pesadas o livianas.

Birds can be heavy
or light.

Estas aves son livianas.

These birds are light.

Los perros pueden ser
pesados o livianos.

Dogs can be heavy
or light.

Estos perros son pesados.

These dogs are heavy.

Las rocas pueden ser
pesadas o livianas.

Rocks can be heavy
or light.

Estas rocas son pesadas.

These rocks are heavy.

Los camiones de verdad
son pesados.

Real trucks are heavy.

Los camiones de juguete
son livianos.

Toy trucks are light.

Una manzana es liviana.

- -

One apple is light.

Muchas manzanas
son pesadas.

Many apples are heavy.

Las cosas de tu casa
pueden ser pesadas
o livianas.

Things in your house
can be heavy or light.

Una cama es pesada.

A bed is heavy.

Las cosas de tu escuela
pueden ser pesadas
o livianas.

Things in your school
can be heavy or light.

Un lápiz es liviano.

A pencil is light.

Las cosas del parque
pueden ser pesadas
o livianas.

Things in the park can be
heavy or light.

Las hojas son ligeras.

Leaves are light.

¿Puedes agrupar
estas herramientas?
¿Cuáles son pesadas?
¿Cuáles son livianas?

Can you sort these tools?
Which are heavy?
Which are light?

Please visit our website, www.garethstevens.com. For a free color catalog of all our high-quality books, call toll free 1-800-542-2595 or fax 1-877-542-2596.

Cataloging-in-Publication Data

O'Hara, Nicholas.
Sort It by weight = Peso / by Nicholas O'Hara.
p. cm. — (Sort It out! = Vamos a agrupar por...)
Parallel title: Vamos a agrupar por...
In English and Spanish.
Includes index.
ISBN 978-1-4824-3226-8 (library binding)
1. Weight (Physics) — Measurement — Juvenile literature. 2. Weight judgment — Juvenile literature. I. O'Hara, Nicholas. II. Title.
QC106.O43 2016
530.8—d23

First Edition

Published in 2016 by
Gareth Stevens Publishing
111 East 14th Street, Suite 349
New York, NY 10003

Designer: Sarah Liddell
Editor: Therese Shea
Spanish Translation: Eida de la Vega

Photo credits: Cover, p. 1 (polka dots) Victoria Kalinina/Shutterstock.com; cover, p. 1 (background, dog, and cat) PHOTOCREO Michal Bednarek/Shutterstock.com; cover, p. 1 (bird and butterfly) Butterfly Hunter/Shutterstock.com; cover, p. 1 (bunny) Stefan Petru Andronache/Shutterstock.com; pp. 3 (basketball, soccer balls, baseball, ping pong balls, and golf balls), 16 (towels) Africa Studio/Shutterstock.com; p. 3 (bowling ball) Pincarel/Shutterstock.com; p. 3 (beach ball) koosen/Shutterstock.com; p. 4 Vaclav Volrab/Shutterstock.com; p. 5 mexrix/Shutterstock.com; p. 6 (ostrich) Aaron Amat/Shutterstock.com; p. 6 (chicks) Eric Isselee/Shutterstock.com; p. 7 WIBOON WIRATTHANAPHAN/Shutterstock.com; p. 8 Erik Lam/Shutterstock.com; p. 9 Susan Schmitz/Shutterstock.com; p. 10 (left) yamix/Shutterstock.com; p. 10 (right) aaltair/Shutterstock.com; p. 11 Tricia Daniel/Shutterstock.com; p. 12 Masekesam/Shutterstock.com; p. 13 yanikap/Shutterstock.com; p. 14 Alex Staroseltsev/Shutterstock.com; p. 15 Photoexpert/Shutterstock.com; p. 16 Kostsov/Shutterstock.com; p. 17 Maksym Bondarchuk/Shutterstock.com; p. 18 Ansis Klucis/Shutterstock.com; p. 19 rzstudio/Shutterstock.com; p. 20 Anatoliy Kosolapov/Shutterstock.com; pp. 20 (leaves), 21 Elena Schweitzer/Shutterstock.com; p. 23 STILLFX/Shutterstock.com.

Printed in the United States of America

CPSIA compliance information: Batch #CS15GS: For further information contact Gareth Stevens, New York, New York at 1-800-542-2595.